THE

FIRST DISCOVERY OF AMERICA,

AND ITS EARLY CIVILIZATION.

TRANSLATED AND ENLARGED FROM THE GERMAN OF
DR. F. KRÜGER,

BY

W. L. WAGENER,

PROFESSOR OF LATIN AND GERMAN IN PACKER COLLEGIATE INSTITUTE, BROOKLYN.

"Nescire autem, quid antequam natus sis acciderit id est, semper esse puerum."—Cicero (*Orator*).

NEW YORK:
SHELDON & COMPANY,
335 BROADWAY, COR. WORTH ST.

1863.

TO

THE TRUSTEES

OF

PACKER COLLEGIATE INSTITUTE, BROOKLYN,

THIS LITTLE WORK

IS MOST RESPECTFULLY DEDICATED AS A

TOKEN OF ESTEEM

BY THE

AUTHOR.

PREFACE.

There appeared several years ago, in the city of Dresden, two Archæological Essays in a German newspaper of the highest literary and scientific character, written by Dr. F. Kruger, and re-published in 1858 in the well-known New York Belletristic Journal.

As there does not exist a reproduction of them in the English language, I have endeavored to supply the deficiency. To the material contained therein large additions—the results of my own researches — have been made. My grateful acknowledgments are due to a lady of Brooklyn for kindly revising the manuscript.

That this little work may meet with a favorable reception from the classical reader, is the earnest wish of the writer.

CONTENTS.

ESSAY I.

ESSAY II.

ESSAY I.

THE FIRST DISCOVERY OF AMERICA.

I.

THE FIRST DISCOVERY OF AMERICA.

THERE are, as is well known, two opinions entertained by literary men concerning the origin of the Aborigines of this country; the one, that they emigrated from the old continent, the other, that they originated in America. The former has been generally received as the true one, and especially relied upon by religious writers; the latter belongs only to modern times. We consider the former the only rational one. The old and the new continents are so near each other, separated only by Behring's Straits, that the necessity of an independent creation of a race on this continent does not exist. And this is more distinctly visible when we take into consideration the fact that the animal and vegetable productions are undeniably American in their origin, until we ascend the scale to human beings, we find the latter bearing a close resemblance to the wild and roving tribes of the old world. The inferior animals, even those which most nearly approach humanity—the apes—are different from the same species in the old world. Apes differ in the number and structure of the teeth, which form a significant and striking zoological mark. In all the American varieties we find thirty-six teeth, both in living specimens and in the remains of those of primitive ages, while on the old continent they have but thirty-two, the same number that is found in human beings. An immigration by way of Behring's Straits is not only natural in itself, but has received the corroboration of strong probability by ethnographical studies and Indian legends. The Esquimaux, who live on both sides of the straits from Kamtschatka to Greenland, and carry on a considerable commerce between the two countries, furnish another significant fact. There is preserved in the Dacotah Indian tribe, on the Mackenzie River, an old tradition that their forefathers came across the ocean from Asia. The Indians of the Mississippi Valley have likewise a tradition which refers to an origin from the north-west.

Important in this connection is the well-known typical resemblance between the great mass of American aborigines and the Mongolian race. On account of this resemblance some of the most learned naturalists have included both races in one. The position here assumed finds additional support when we examine the evidences of early civilization found throughout the whole continent, especially in Central and South America.

The great variety of languages in America, as well as in the remaining parts of the world, has raised the question whether the emigrants from Asia brought their language and culture with them, or whether they were wholly barbarous, and by their own mental power were able to bring themselves to that state of cultivation in which they were found when conquered by the Spaniards. Against the latter opinion there have been for a long period eminent objections.

First of all deserves to be mentioned the opinion of Alexander von Humboldt, the prince of learned men, at which he arrived about sixty years ago, while engaged in scientific pursuits in America, and explained in one of his most interesting works.* He refers to the most surprising relations existing between the culture of Eastern Asia and ancient America, especially seen in the arrangement of the calendar, which could not possibly depend on mere casualty, and judges that there must have been an emigration from Japan and Eastern Asia generally. This opinion is considered the more tenable one because it entirely agrees with the above-mentioned typical affinity between the Amer-

* Vues des Cordillères et Monumens des Peuples indigènes de l'Amérique (Paris, 1810).

ican aborigines and the inhabitants of Eastern Asia.

In the course of the last five decades, however, there appears a victorious opinion in historical science—*i. e.*, of a self-creation of culture from the nation's own mind, which, however, we consider exaggerated.

There was found in America a wide difference in the degrees of culture which characterized the aboriginal inhabitants, a portion or whom were wild, rude, and barbarous, without knowledge of law or form of government, while others were more mild in character, reproducing somewhat the conditions of pastoral life in the old country, or of that transition state from the pastoral to the agricultural life. Yet, strange as it may seem, the ancient Mexicans had no knowledge of domestic animals.

It is most improbable that the ancient Americans raised themselves by their own power from the entirely rude condition of wild Indians to such a high degree of culture.

Accordingly, therefore, the opinion of Humboldt is to be retained as of value, and indeed we see no reason why we should contradict its important arguments.

The mode of civilization in America was, however, so varied, that the adoption of the theory of an origin from but one region is entirely unnecessary. There exists, also, among the inhabitants a typical contrast, which renders a scientific solution necessary.

Besides the resemblance to the Mongolian race, which is considerable, there exists, according to the observation of people who have resided for a long time in the northern part of South America, but a slight difference between the immigrated Chinese Coolies and the native Indians in regard to their physiognomy and structure of the body. So, also, there appears in the once highly-cultivated Central American a type in its purity quite contrary to the Mongolian, which learned men, who observed it in that part of the continent, have pronounced "Semitic." To this

Semitic race belonged also the very ancient people of Babylonia, which possessed the whole plain of Middle Asia. Their language was spoken in many dialects on that side of the Halys River (now called Kisil-Irmark) on the western coast of Asia Minor, prevailing from the Tigris as far as the Caucasian Mountains and the southern point of Arabia. The Phœnicians, as well as their Carthaginian descendants, belonged to this Semitic race.

This observation caused an opinion to circulate, in itself childlike, referring to a Judaical origin of the Indians. This opinion prevails among the North American people, and, according to the reports of Scherzer, among the cultivated inhabitants of Central America and Mexico. It is not only one of the most important dogmas of the Mormon religion, but even English scholars used much diligence and sagacity to make it appear that the lost ten tribes of Israel arrived in America in some natural manner, and there became the fathers of the Indians.

While we intend to solve this ethnographical problem, we pronounce it from the beginning as our opinion that, as well in early antiquity as since the fifteenth century, the Atlantic Ocean offered the way of communication which made possible a mingling of both systems of culture of the old and new continents. This opinion is not at all new; but as its former defenders cited only a few points in their arguments, they did not succeed in giving to them sufficient strength.

As we intend to investigate this question thoroughly, we will undertake a new comparison of both the witnesses of the ancients concerning a large continent beyond the Atlantic Ocean, and also the mutual accordance of the two continents in religion and culture—finally, the traditions of the American aborigines, and we trust to be able to adduce in favor of our opinion arguments not only new but by their interior harmony convincing also. We commence with the witnesses of the ancients.

The opinion that large masses of land are hidden in the Western Ocean, was so often pronounced by the authors of antiquity, that in the days of reviving literature the minds of the first discoverers were most actively incited and determined. Especially by the saying of Seneca in his tragedy "Medea:"

> "Late centuries will appear,
> When the ocean's vails will lift
> To open a vast country.
> New worlds will unvail Thethys.
> Thule will not remain the earth's boundary."

Thethys is the poetical name for "the Atlantic Ocean," and Thule for "Iceland." The old Romans called it also "Ultima Thule," *i. e.* "the last, the remotest Thule."

Alexander von Humboldt proved this influence in the most unequivocal way, and analyzed from this point of view many ancient judgments.

While we are giving this point of view a similar examination, we must distinguish first of all between such passages as, relying upon the theory of the spherical form of the earth, declare only a scientific conviction, and those which contain a distinct tradition of a discovery by the maritime nations. Such reports can, of course, have the authority of real traditions only when they

Firstly, show geographical communications which agree with the real condition of the new world; and

Secondly, if they in themselves contain sufficient historical probability.

For such witnesses we are indebted to the Greek authors, Plutarch, Diodorus Siculus, and Aristotle. It shall be our endeavor to show how far they can claim scientific consideration.

We commence with a passage from Plutarch, in his treatise, "De Facie in Orbe Lunæ," which is very important, since it seems to contain an unequivocal description of America.

Plutarch is citing a Sylla speaking in the following manner:

1. "When there is no objection to it I begin Homeric:

. "An island is lying far Ogygia (far in the ocean), five days' voyage from Britain, as one sails westward.

2. "Three others stand at equal distances from each other, and lie very far toward the hot sunset.

3. "On one of them, the barbarians have the fable, Chronos was once confined, having his son as watchman. He now lives beyond those islands and the ocean, which is called 'Chronic Ocean.'

4. "The vast continent, which is surrounded by the large ocean, lies not far from the island—from Ogygia about 5,000 stadia (one stadium equal to 606¾ English feet). Only rowing vessels are used to approach it, for the ocean is penetrable with difficulty, and muddy, on account of the continent washing down slime, so that the ocean is sluggish and earthy, for which reason one imagines it as dense.

5. "On the continent Hellenians live around the bay, which is not smaller than the 'Palus Mæotis' (now called the Sea of Azof). Those people call and consider themselves 'Continentals;' the inhabitants of our country, however, since it is encircled by the ocean, they call 'Islanders.'

6. "They believe the attendants of Hercules had mixed themselves with the people of Chronos, and having been left behind, had again inflamed, invigorated and enlarged the Greek character, which was almost expired—well-nigh extinguished by barbarian language, laws, and manners of living. Therefore Hercules has the greatest honors, but Chronos the next ones.

7. "When the constellation of Chronos, which the Hellenians call the fire constellation, they, however, 'Nycturos,' enters the Taurus, which happens every thirty years, they send on a voyage persons previously chosen by lot, who have been preparing themselves for a long time for this sacrifice and

journey. The vessels, servants, and equipments are the same as if they were going to cross a vast ocean with the oar, and had resolved to remain abroad a long time.

8. "Those who have departed have now a different destiny; those who are spared by the ocean, land at first at the foremost islands inhabited by Hellenians, where, for thirty days, the sun disappears less than one hour, and the night brings only slight darkness, as if surrounded with twilight.

9. "After a sojourn of ninety days, and having been treated honorably and friendly, they are conveyed home again by the winds, after having been considered and announced as 'saints.' No other people live there besides themselves and those who were before sent thither. For those who have served out the thirty years to the god are allowed to sail homeward. The greatest part of them prefer to remain, some of them because they are acclimated, others because they are relieved from labor and occupation,

and every thing exists in abundance for immolations, choragi, and for engaging in sciences or in philosophy.

10. "For the island is worthy to be admired for the beauty of its natural scenery and the mildness of the encircling breeze. To some of the voyagers the tutelary god becomes an impediment. When they are about to depart, he shows himself to them and to their relatives and friends, for many of them, not only by dreams and omens, but also publicly, by vision and voice, have intercourse with the spirits.

11. "In deep cavities slumbers Chronos on the godlike rocks, watched because Zeus has made the sleep like a fetter upon him. Over the top of the rock birds flutter, bearing to him in their bills 'ambrosia.' The whole island is filled with the fragrance of it.

12. "Those are spirits waiting upon Chronos and serving him, since they have been during his government over mankind and gods his joys. Many things they divine from

their own prophetic inspiration, the sublimest, however, they announce as dreams of Chronos.

13. "For whatever Zeus foresees appears to Chronos in a dream. When he awakes, then rises his Titanic rage and the passions of his soul, which were oppressed by sleep, so his royal and divine character appears again pure and clear.

14. "After having arrived here, as he said, the guest, who served the god at leisure, acquired such a knowledge of astrology as it would be possible for an astronomical scholar of the highest proficiency, since among other philosophical branches the natural sciences were cultivated.

15. "He departed after thirty years had passed away, and the successors had arrived from home with the desire to see the large island, as our continent is said to be called; having been dismissed by his friends without much baggage, but with a strong traveling provision of golden goblets, *i. e.*, wine.

16. "What occurred to him now, how many people he met, what he thought of the holy sciences, into how many mysteries he was initiated, and with what else he became acquainted, can not be related in one day; neither can that which entered into the particulars of his recollection. What, however, concerns the present subject you shall hear.

17. "In Carthage he spent the longest time, and found some parchment rolls buried among the ruins of the ancient city, for a long time concealed in the earth. He recommended me to entertain a distinguished veneration for those gods appearing in the universe, for instance, 'Selene' (the Greek name for 'moon'), since she has the greatest right of our life." Those are the passages of Plutarch.

According to our promise we will submit them point after point to an examination, and also compare the traditions of the Mexicans with many of the intimations contained therein.

In the beginning it is said: "Ogygia lies toward the west from Britain, three other islands in front of it very far toward the hot sun." The last passage gives us a hint where we must look for those islands—evidently in the tropical Central America. Here, among many islands, four are especially observable, which in their magnitude and beauty excel all the others, *i. e.*, Cuba, Jamaica, Hayti, and Porto Rico. They are from each other almost equidistant, just as Plutarch reports. The five days' voyage is an error upon which nobody will lay any stress who is acquainted with and has examined the statements which Greek geographers make in regard to distances. As for instance, Onesicrotos, in giving the distance of Ceylon from the Indian continent, makes it twenty days' voyage, a ridiculous statement to us, since we know that the real distance is thirty-two English miles. But as an intelligent man will draw from this a conclusion that the ancients knew nothing about Ceylon, so little, also, is the above five days' voyage a counterproof against the acquaintance of the ancients with America. According to paragraph third, Chronos was confined by Zeus on one of the islands. As is known, there was in all antiquity, and also in America, a common belief that earthquakes are generated by giants and gods who have been confined by other superior beings and buried under mountains. So Zeus is said to have heaped Etna upon the Titans; so was the Persian Zobac fettered by Feridun under the Demawend; so the German Loce conquered and tied in a cavern of the interior of the earth by the power of the twelve Asen (deities of both sexes). We have, therefore, in the above passages nothing but an allegorical rendering of the sentence: "One of these islands is of a volcanic character, exposed to earthquakes and eruptions." These latter are common, as is known, in the whole of Central America. Active volcanoes exist, especially on the Caribbean Islands, in abundance, and various hints in the writers of antiquity show us that they were never missed in the four islands mentioned, where they are yet to be found.

Still more distinctly, yes, as distinctly as one can describe, is stated in the fourth paragraph:

"A large continent is here spoken of, which is surrounded by a large ocean; it is at a less distance from the other islands, but from Ogygia it is 5,000 stadia. By the multitude of streams which wash down mud and slime the ocean is rendered thick and earthy."

It is certainly impossible not to perceive in this a description of the American continent. That embraces a large archipelago, the Gulf of Mexico, and the Caribbean Sea. It sends forth many rivers—as the Mississippi, the Rio del Norte, the Magdalene River, the Orinoco, which together are heaping up an alluvial deposit more important than the celebrated delta formations of the Nile. Not only by these alluvions but by many banks, as that of the Honduras and the large ones of Bahamas, is the navigation rendered difficult in manifold ways.

How exact altogether the whole descriptions are one can perceive by reading Voelcker's "Book of Geography." There stands, for instance, in the second volume:

"The continual current of the sea along the coast from the Peninsula of Yucatan as far as the Straits of Florida, heaps up great masses of sand which are increased by the wash of the rivers that flow into the sea. All the harbors, therefore, along the eastern Mexican coast are utterly unsafe and are exposed to all storms."

Astonishing indeed is the statement of the distance of Ogygia from a spot easily to be recognized as upon this continent. Five thousand stadia are five hundred and fifty English miles, or eight and a half degrees, which is exactly the distance of Cuba from the mouth of the Mississippi River. That this point only can be fixed upon, and not another, appears distinctly in consequence of the mention of large masses of slime washed down and impeding greatly the navigation, by which the delta of the Mississippi River is to be understood. It follows from this that the island which is called by Plutarch "Ogygia," is one and the same with "Cuba" of our day, which deserves of course, as it is by far the largest island of Central America, to be rendered especially prominent.

In paragraph fifth Plutarch reports that the maritime countries of the continent are inhabited by Hellenians settled around a gulf not smaller than the Sea of "Azof." Without doubt this is the Gulf of Mexico, on whose coasts at the time of Cortez still existed the empire of the Aztecs, who immigrated to Anahuak (Mexico) in 1160, A.D., from the unknown northern countries "Aztlan." It is well known what a high degree of culture these people had attained at that period. The ancient scholars supposed this nation to be derived from the Toltec race, who probably immigrated in the seventh century, A.D., from northern countries, and after having conquered almost the whole of Central America reared there many gigantic works of architecture. The newer investigations have proved an existence anterior to the Toltec culture, and doubtless of great age. The Toltec nation existed very probably in Guatemala, Nicaragua, on the Great Antilles, etc., until the time of discovery and later by the name of the "Maja people." The relics likewise of their culture to be found in the territory of the Mississippi River are, according to certain marks, very old.

The statement of Plutarch of a nation already highly cultivated, and living on that gulf of the new world, is in itself not at all improbable. In regard to the additional clause, that the nation was Greek, it is a well-known fact, that the vain Greeks, whenever an unknown cultivated nation was mentioned, always thought at first of themselves.

Their Bœotic Hercules is said to have conquered India, and even more.

Plutarch proceeds to religious expeditions toward the north, to islands where the sun during thirty days disappears less than one hour. The nights are described as polar nights with slight twilight. The whole statement is confused, as it could hardly fail to be, since Plutarch speaks of that of which he has not had the least observation. Afterward he reverts to the island "Chronos," picturing it as a genuine paradise (and what glowing impression the Antilles made upon the Spaniards!) Wonderful are the natural characteristics of the island; the mildness of the breeze, the brilliant birds, sweet aromatics; nothing, indeed, is forgotten which a ravished describer of travels would relate concerning the charms of tropical countries. Mingled with this there is much of mythology, which, however, is spoken of in Mexican legends. Plutarch introduces a native of America who, animated by a desire to see the large island (as Plutarch's Americans called the eastern continent), had sailed with a great store of golden goblets, *i. e.*, wine, toward the east, and had landed in Carthage, where he staid for a long time. That an American native could, at Plutarch's day, arrive in Carthage by way of the Atlantic Ocean is so little conformable to our prejudices, that it appears quite ridiculous. Nevertheless, when we candidly contemplate the relation of Plutarch we find nothing which is absolutely untrue. Among all the deities of the universe he makes his guest pay veneration to the goddess of the moon. Throughout ancient America the moon was highly prominent above all others. It is remarkable that Carthage is also mentioned in connection with two other statements about a large country lying in the Atlantic Ocean.

The first of these references is to be found in the author Diodorus Siculus. In the nineteenth and twentieth chapters of the fifth book he says: "After describing the islands within the columns of Hercules, we pass to those in the ocean. Opposite to Africa lies an island, in the midst of the ocean, which on account of its magnitude is worthy to be mentioned. It is several days' voyage distant from Africa, has a fertile soil, many mountains, and not a few plains unexcelled in their beauty. It is watered by navigable rivers, possesses many paradises planted with various kinds of trees, and also gardens in abundance, intersected by sweet streams. There are to be found farms adorned with artistic buildings, and in the gardens are cottages, in which the inhabitants spend the hot season of the year. The hilly country has thick and extensive forests and various fruit-trees, and the valleys between the mountains offer refreshing and copious fountains. The chase is rich in every kind of game, and therefore the inhabitants are not in want of any thing which may contribute to revels and pomp. The sea, which washes the shores is crowded with fish, like in character to those of the ocean, which also contains them in abundance. A multitude of hard-rinded and other fruits are to be had through the greater part of the year. Indeed it appears, on account of the great abundance of its charms, as if it were the sojourn of gods and not of human beings."

These and the following passages are so precise, that they can not be called either mythic or trite. The question reduces itself to this, whether the island of Diodorus be America, or whether it be one of the Canaries or Azores. The latter opinion meets with decided objections. In the first place Diodorus calls it considerably large, and the Azores and Canaries are but small. Diodorus attributes to the island navigable rivers, while on the Azores there are only brooks. The Canaries, on account of their well-known aridity, still less permit this interpretation. Besides, the island of Diodorus has very extensive plains, and the islands of the Atlantic Ocean are—as is well-known—without exception mere peaks of submarine mountains. In every respect the description of Diodorus agrees with that one of Plutarch of the Island "Ogygia." The statement of both authors respecting the distance from Africa refers to the relations of that far Western country with the neighboring cluster of islands, of which the Canaries were certainly known in remote antiquity. The coincidence between Plutarch and Diodorus nearly confines the interpretation to the largest island of Central America.

Cuba has a hundred and fifty running streams, among which Sagua Grande and Rio Cauto are in fact navigable. The greater part of the surface of the country consists of mountains, which rise to the altitude of 8,400 feet. A not less noticeable part extends itself in plains especially in those river valleys near the ocean. The condition of that Western country as here described corresponds sufficiently well with that of America, for a precise analysis in such reports can never be expected. Those farms adorned with magnificent buildings also indicate "America." The degree of civilization, which at the time of the discovery existed on the large Antilles, was only the relic of a declining and formerly far higher culture, as is seen from certain marks. The expressions which Diodorus uses about the richness of the soil, fitting the country for a habitation of gods rather than of human beings, occur likewise in passages of the first Spanish discoverers and missionaries, whose reports relate:

"The multitude of paradises with all sorts of trees planted therein, gardens with sweet rivulets intersecting them, the frequent and luxuriant tropical forests, the wonderful mildness of the climate, which causes the earth to produce through the longest part of the year a multitude of hard-rinded and other fruits, can not sufficiently be praised."

In the following chapter of Diodorus the

way of the discovery by the Phœnicians is related:

"In early antiquity it was unknown through its remoteness from the whole habitable world, at a later day it was discovered in consequence of the following circumstances: The Phœnicians having from the most ancient times incessantly made commercial journeys, established in Africa many colonies no less than in Europe, and in the regions toward the sunset. As their enterprises succeeded to their wish, they gained great riches. Afterward they ventured to sail, passed the columns of Hercules into the ocean, after having founded on the straits between the columns a city, and called it Gadeira (Cadiz). Besides some others suitable to the locality, they erected a splendid temple to Hercules, and sacrificed gorgeous victims conformably to their rites. This temple was highly venerated in ancient times, and also in later centuries, even till our days. While exploring the coast of

Africa on that side of the columns, the Phœnicians were driven by heavy winds far out into the ocean. Tossed about for many days by storms they were carried finally to the aforesaid island, and after investigating its charms, carried home the account. But when the sea-mighty Tyrians were going to send thither a colony, the Carthaginians prevented them, partly out of fear that many would emigrate thither from Carthage, partly in order to keep an asylum in case of some misfortune occurring. In that event they wished to accomplish a universal emigration to that island." This testimony is completed and enlarged by the already-mentioned passage from a work generally ascribed to Aristotle, "De Mirabilibus Auscultationibus Liber." This work is certainly not genuine, but it is at all events older than our chronology. Here it is said:

"In the ocean on the further side of the columns of Hercules have the Carthaginians discovered a waste island distant several days' voyage, provided with woods, navigable rivers, and admirable on account of its productions." Both witnesses, to which a certain historical character can not be denied, agree perfectly in the principal matter. The navigable rivers mentioned by Aristotle prove that he did not refer to the small islands of the Atlantic Ocean.

Diodorus says: "That country, so remote from others, is said to have been discovered by the Phœnicians, but it was known also to the Carthaginians." This does not contradict the report of Aristotle, of its discovery by the latter; it may be that he refers to an after-discovery. Aristotle, however, calls the island, to which Diodorus ascribes a cultivated population, a "waste one." Without doubt he confounds the island (of which Plutarch also speaks) with the continent. There are—as is known—immense tracts of lands, especially in the south, which may be called uninhabited.

The Carthaginian rulers forbade the voyage

to this newly discovered country under pain of death, and killed all the emigrants, in order that they might not promulgate the knowledge of its existence, lest that then the island should gain the predominance, and injure the prosperity of the mother country. The rulers of the Carthaginians were—as is known—rich, moneyed aristocrats, whose authority and importance, as everywhere in our own days, depended on the work of an enormous multitude of paupers. Therefore by an emigration in mass their prosperity would be ruined as well as that of the state itself, whose power was founded upon the density of its population. The matters of fact which are contained in the reports of Diodorus and Aristotle certainly contradict all our prejudices. But when they are submitted to investigation, they appear not improbable. They are moreover sustained by important historical and geographical arguments.

That the Phœnicians in ancient time navigated the Atlantic Ocean is a well-known fact. It is hardly less certain that they had a not inconsiderable commercial intercourse with the western coast of Africa, which continent they had completely circumnavigated, according to an entirely reliable report of Herodotus. The Greek author Strabo relates also that the Carthaginians possessed on the African coast a hundred colonies, which is an evidence of an active commerce with tropical Africa. There are in the Atlantic ocean-currents and also currents of air north of the equator; they are of such a character, that an active navigation in those regions hardly can take place without leading by mere accident to America. It is known that it was a tradewind, in connection with equatorial currents, which opened Brazil to the Portuguese under Cabral in 1500 A.D., without any intention on their part. Is it then surprising if a similar eastern storm should have driven, according to Diodorus, a Phœnician, and according to Aristotle, a Carthaginian vessel toward the west, and opened to it the American continent? One is accustomed to lay too great stress upon the lack of the compass. In the above case this would rather favor the discovery, when the navigators, driven away from the land, and having entirely lost their course, sailed perhaps toward the west, while the compass would have directed them eastward.

In pleasant weather heaven is the best leader, therefore was the return not a difficult matter. When they perceived that they had been carried toward the west, they had only to sail back in a plain eastern direction, in order to reach Spain again. (Columbus in his voyage of discovery kept an almost straight direction.)

It is highly improbable that the discovery of a country so rich in resources of all kinds should not have stimulated to the utmost activity a nation of so much boldness and enterprise as the Phœnician Carthaginians! Our excellent Movers has clearly shown in the last volume of his Phœnician Archaeology, how little foundation there is for our prejudices in regard to the ship-building of the ancients. He proves positively that the ship-building of the Phœnicians was much more perfect and practical than that of the Romans, Greeks, and of the Europeans before the latest discovery of America. Surely their ships were not worse than those three infirm vessels with which Columbus sailed from the Spanish harbor Palos near Cadiz. For the rest one must not attach too much importance to such technical auxiliary means, since the chief lever for great actions is found in the power and activity of the people. The Northmen discovered in their open boats, without any other leader than the heavens, not only Iceland in the year 861 A.D., but even America in the tenth century, as it is stated in the archives of the city of Copenhagen. There was some years ago in the neighborhood of the town of Fall River, R. I., dug up a skeleton in complete Scandinavian armor. It is a certain historical fact, that Greenland and Vinland (probably Labrador of our days) were known at that time, and even the coast of Massachusetts (Boston), and Florida also. (There existed there a bishopric, which had sent teeth of river-horses [hippopotami] as tribute to Rome.) Since the end of the fourteenth century this knowledge had been lost, and in the fifteenth century, the century of voyages and discovery, nothing was thought of but how to find a passage to the East Indies by way of the Western Ocean. The Northmen navigated on all southern seas, as far as the Canary Islands. There is also the circumnavigation of Africa by the Phœnicians, of which we possess such respectable proof. This is by no means easier than the voyage to America, as we may see by considering the expeditions of Columbus and his followers. Again, the voyage of the Phœnicians to America is not to be compared to the circumnavigation of the globe by Magellan, 1519–1522, even if we lay peculiar stress upon the real or pretended inferiority of nautical auxiliary means in Phœnician antiquity. The Portuguese were obliged with very slender equipment to cross the Pacific, to which the Atlantic, as regards extent and fearful solitude, can not be compared.

For the rest the relations of the Phœnicians to the Pacific and Atlantic Ocean were like those of the northern Europeans to the Atlantic and Pacific.

Among all the accounts in history concerning the large western country lying beyond the Atlantic Ocean, none is more interesting and important than the account of Plato, the pupil of Socrates, of the "Atlantis."

In his dialogues, "Timæus and Critias," the great philosopher relates that Solon had during his stay in Egypt conversed much with the Saitic priests upon the most prominent questions of human science, and the priests had told him of a nation which in the most ancient times, before the Hellenians, had dwelt in Greece and also in Africa.

Concerning it they spoke thus :

"The books report of a mighty power which had once well-nigh destroyed your state. At that time the sea was navigable; it had an island lying before its mouth, which you call as you assert, 'the Columns of Hercules.' From this island, which was larger than Africa and Asia together, one could reach other islands, and from those the whole opposite continent around that real ocean. On this island, 'Atlantis,' existed a great and memorable royal power, which governed also many islands and parts of the continent. Besides it ruled over the countries within the straits over the coasts of Africa as far as Egypt, and over Europe as far as Etruria. This power once undertook to reduce to slavery the inhabitants of our, your, and all the remaining countries within the straits, which design, however, was frustrated by the Uratenians through a heroic fortitude excelling that of all their contemporaries. In later times however, by great earthquakes and inundations, in one day and one night of misfortune, your whole army was devoured by the earth, and the island 'Atlantis' by the ocean. Therefore the sea is now inaccessible and unexplored, since the deep morass left behind by the disappearance of the island prevents all navigation."

There is no sufficient cause for doubting the Egyptian origin of the myth, which was transmitted by Solon to Timæus and the Critias, and by them to a contemporary of Plato, or even to Plato himself. The Egyptians could however easily have obtained news of the remote West from their Phœnician neighbors. As a prominent point in the dialogue we notice the mention of an immense morass in the Atlantic Ocean as an impediment to the navigation. "Critias" argues that the ancient Egyptians, and accordingly the Phœnicians, were well acquainted with the vast Fucus Banks lying in the midst of the ocean, and indeed north-west of the Azores. We are almost constrained to this belief when we examine Columbus' report of his first expedition. He says: "I found the sea covered with such a mass of weeds, that I was forced to believe the vessels would come upon a shallow for a lack of water. No trace, however, was to be perceived of such sea-plants anywhere else."

The idea that the ancients in their voyages only skirted the coasts is therefore refuted by this statement, which forms likewise an evidence that they were acquainted with the much nearer Azores, for Plato says:

"One can pass over from that great island to the remaining islands, and from these to continent."

The remaining islands can be no others than the Azores, and perhaps also the Canaries, which are still intermediate stages between the old and the new continents. It follows not less from the account of Plato than from those of Plutarch, Diodorus, and Aristotle, that this large western country can not be any of the minor islands of the ocean, *but simply the American continent.*

The story of the destruction of the island "Atlantis" (after which the western ocean was probably named by the ancients, "Atlantic Ocean") can be explained thus: There existed perhaps in the primitive time an island of moderate extent, which was destroyed by such a catastrophe. Since such an intermediate stage would have facilitated the intercourse with America, the opinion might easily arise after its destruction, that the continent lying behind had been also destroyed. From a scientific point of view such a catastrophe is not improbable. The island of Ferdinandea arose suddenly between Africa and Sicily, but afterward was swept away. At the mouth of the Indus, after an earthquake in 1819, a tract of land of almost a hundred square miles disappeared, and the spot is now occupied by a large lake. The bed of the Atlantic Ocean is decidedly of volcanic character. The islands which it contains, the Azores, Canaries, and Cape Verde, have burning volcanos. The volcanos of the Caribbean Islands are in constant activity. That horrible earthquake which destroyed Lisbon in 1755, stirred up the whole ocean from the Antilles as far as Greenland. The American earthquakes in 1811–13 were felt as far as the Azores.

This interpretation disagrees however with the above-discussed testimonies of three Greek authors, Plutarch, Diodorus, and Aristotle, who mention no destruction of the islands of which they speak.

More probable therefore may be the following explanation :

"The Phœnicians, endowed above other nations with intelligence, energy, and enterprise, had in the early days of their greatness (1000–600 B.C.) discovered America.

The following generations, encouraged by reports of that old intercourse, attempted likewise the great navigation across the Atlantic Ocean. They went, however, only as far as the vast Fucus prairies. Since they did not venture to sail beyond them, they invented after their return the fiction of the destruction of that large western country, and of the morass left behind by its sinking. With respect to the great political power of those islands, which are said to have subjugated whole empires in Europe and Africa, we can find no mention of it in any historical tradition. It is, however, remarkable that in the most ancient times a highly cultivated nation has inhabited the whole of North America as far as the five lakes, *i. e.*, Lake Superior, Michigan, Huron, Erie, and Ontario, and that many remains of fortified cities, temples, and pyramids prove its existence and greatness. There was discovered in 1787, near the large Indian village Palenque (in Southern Mexico, in the State of Chiapa), the considerable ruins of the ancient city of Colhuacan, which must have had an extent of over twelve miles. There are still to be seen ruins of palaces, temples, walls with semi-relief of sculpture and human beings portrayed of quite another race than that found by the Europeans in 1500. There were also found hieroglyphics which were unmistakably Egyptian in their character. In the States of Georgia, Kentucky (in the Mammoth Cave even mummies were discovered), Iowa, Ohio, and many others exist fortifications of earth dating from an ante-Indian period, and many other monuments of very primitive ages. It is also certain that this culture did not arise in the valley of the Mississippi, but was introduced from the South. This is to be seen by the representations on monuments of southern animals and plants not existing in North America.

We have therefore to distinguish three different discoveries of America:

The first one during the period from 1000–600 B.C., by the Phœnicians and their Carthaginian descendants.

The second one in the tenth century A.D., by the Northmen and Scandinavians, and

The third one in 1492, by the Genoese Christopher Columbus.

ESSAY II.

THE COINCIDENCES AND RELATIONS OF ANCIENT AMERICAN AND ORIENTAL CULTURE.

II.

THE COINCIDENCES AND RELATIONS OF ANCIENT AMERICAN AND ORIENTAL CULTURE.

THE testimony of the authors of antiquity, which we considered in the preceding essay, furnishes a complete solution of the problem, how it is possible that one part of the ancient inhabitants of America should exhibit a typical affinity with the Semitic race.

To this Semitic race belonged the most ancient inhabitants of Babylonia, who possessed the whole plain of Middle Asia. Their language was spoken in many dialects, from the Halys River to the Tigris, and from the Caucasian Mountains to the southern point of Arabia. The Phœnicians and their Carthaginian descendants belonged also to the Semitic race.

It is now the question, whether the ancient culture of America is of a kind that can be referred to a partially Semitic origin or not. It is a matter of fact that in the whole mode of civilization, and also in the mythology, there is such analogical proof of relation to the Phœnicians, and especially to the ancient Egyptians, that even the most zealous defenders of the theory of an indigenous culture are obliged to concede its importance.

Before we investigate this conformity in detail, we may be permitted to cast a glance at those nations of antiquity to which first of all we must refer. It is a wrong custom with modern historians, to search for the origin of human culture among the ancient Greeks. It arises from the want of historical knowledge of other nations of antiquity, and from the influence of prejudice. By the more recent investigations in Oriental literature it is seen that the Greek mode of civilization was the only one possible to a nation whose prosperity commenced when that of the whole remaining world presented the spectacle of an immense decay, and that that age, contemplated as a whole, can be esteemed only as a period of decay or decline. It was preceded by other ages of a most flourishing condition of Western Asia, during which that part of the world exerted no less influence on the commercial and national relations of the globe than Europe now does. Just as Europe does now, so Western Asia manifested its superior force for two thousand years B.C. One proof of this is seen in the European languages which almost all evince an Oriental origin. Rome, Carthage, Etruria, and Hispania were, as we know from certain tradition, colonies of Western Asia. The Phœnicians established and ruled colonies on almost all the coasts of the Mediterranean Sea. The culture of this sacerdotal age of the world became far extended by the Britons and others, who in the earliest historical age emigrated, partially by way of Egypt, to the western countries.

Fifteen or sixteen centuries B.C. the Egyptians waged wars of conquest which, according to several authors, extended their power as far as Bactria, and even India. Their culture had already advanced in a remarkable degree, and their monuments give proof that many of the hostile nations were hardly lower in the scale of intellectual development.

In later times the Iranic nation, consisting of the Aledians and the Persians, threw off the Egyptian yoke, and undertook a campaign toward the northern part of Africa, by means of which they left behind, as Sallust reports—quoting from Carthaginian books—colonies in Spain and Africa.

The Greek author, Diodorus Siculus, reports that Egypt from the most ancient times was not spared by foreign conquerors. He speaks of the Hycsos, pastoral kings, who residing in Memphis, governed for centuries, and erected the great pyramid near Cairo, which reached the altitude of 450 feet. At that time the Jews were captives in Egypt. These Hycsos are said to have been of Arabian descent. Then Diodorus speaks of the Ethiopian Sabaco, whose prey Egypt became for a long time. Sabaco invaded Egypt in 750 B. C., and kept it for fifty years.

To the Semitic culture belongs as a capital branch the very ancient hierarchical culture of Etruria. Not less similar to it is that of ancient Spain. The Etruscans possessed the country from the Tiber as far as the Alps about 1490 B.C., had established colonies in Southern Italy and on the smaller islands of the Mediterranean Sea, and at the time of the Trojan war were noted for their commerce, navigation, and knowledge of other secular as well as religious affairs. The Romans borrowed many of their institutions from them. But before they were able to develop the beautiful shoots of their culture, the Gauls from beyond the Alps invaded and took from them the whole valley of the Po. Their settlements in the South became the prey of the Samnites, and at last they were subjugated by the Romans. Like the most of the nations of that time they had not organized themselves into separate states. When they came in contact with the Romans, they possessed twelve cities, each with a dependent territory in Etruria. Each of these had a Lucumo, which means "a man of the laws." These Lucumos are analogous to the Carthaginian Suffetes. At an early age the arts and sciences flourished among them. Their tasteful vases still serve our artists as models. Their flourishing condition lasted from 1077–670 B.C., when Rome arose, and took away one city after another.

In modern times were dug up in Tarragona (Spain) walls of very ancient buildings, which prove by their sculpture that in Spain as well as in Egypt hieroglyphics supplied the place of written letters. On the Canary Islands, especially on Teneriffe, there existed laws and sacerdotal institutions quite similar to those of the Egyptians. In particular the embalming of the dead was a striking feature.

Mr. Jones in his excellent history of Ancient America (London, 1843, Vol. I.), speaks of the mummies found on the Canaries as follows:

"Mummies have been discovered (but without the sarcophagi) at Arico, in the island of Teneriffe, and at Arica in Peru—a similitude is discernible even in the local name given to the districts, where the mummy-pits were found. Analogy is at once perceptible in analyzing the ancient word Guanches (the aborigines of Teneriffe). It is derived from Guan—*i. e.*, man, consequently in his natural and uncontrolled state—therefore Freemen—this fact is sanctioned by their escape from thralldom or slavery, when they first arrived on the island.

Again, in ancient America the places where mummies are found are called Guacas, *i. e.*, the abode of man in his decayed state. The reader will instantly perceive that in the construction of the word as used in both localities, there is a direct similitude. The first land also re-discovered by Columbus in the western hemisphere, was called by the natives Guanahani—the Genoese named it St. Salvador.

The word "Teneriffe" in the original language of the ancient inhabitants—the Guanches—signifies White Mountains (Thanar, mountain, and Iffe, white), from the celebrated peak being (from its altitude) always covered with snow. The word "mummy" was originally applied to a drug so called, which was probably used by the Egyptians as one of their ingredients in embalming or preserving the dead. It may appear strange at the first glance that there should be any connection between the mummies of Teneriffe and those of Peru toward establishing that the American aborigines were originally Tyrians; but there is a connection, and as certain as that a chain of three links owes its utility to the connecting power of the central one, Teneriffe forms that central link between Tyrus and the western continent. The natural question then is—Were the Guanches (ancient Canarians) of the Tyrian family?—This we distinctly answer in the affirmative.

Mr. Pettigrew, in his valuable "History of Egyptian Mummies," has the following remark upon those discovered at Teneriffe: "That the inhabitants of the Canary Islands should have adopted a practice of embalming in some measure similar to that of the Egyptian is rather singular, seeing that they were separated from each other by the entire breadth of North Africa." Now the above author assumes as a necessity that the ancient Guanches (Canarians) must have emigrated by land; otherwise the sentence "entire breadth of Northern Africa" is uselessly brought forward to express the barrier between the islands and Egypt. The theory of the emigration by land cannot be sustained, but it is absolutely rejected and interdicted by the fact that the Guanches must have had means of navigation in order to have reached the chief islands, even after their arrival upon the shores of the continent —which are nearly one hundred and fifty miles from Teneriffe. This fact, then, points to a nation having acquaintance with Egypt and the means of navigation; and also of one "advanced in civilization," for such were the now extinct nation of Guanches, as described by the Spanish historians. Truth seems at once to point to the Tyrians as the aborigines of those islands. Mr. Pettigrew probably forgot that Herodotus has recorded the celebrated Egypto-Tyrian expedition around the continent of Africa, which occurred 609–606 years B.C. It is apparent that the Fortunatæ Insulæ, as the Canary Islands were called by the ancients, were discovered during the three years' voyage related by the Greek historian, for they were known to the Tyrians centuries before the Christian era. After the direful event (*i. e.*, the destruction of Tyre by Alexander the Great) which drove the Tyrians forever from the Mediterranean, we believe that their first resting-place was among the Canary Islands—and as the Peak of Teneriffe arose as a welcome beacon—that island became to them the chief place of temporary residence after their fortunate escape. It appears quite evident that the group was then named by the Tyrians—for as the Fortunate Isles they are known in ancient geography.

That the aborigines of the islands and those of ancient America were the same will be admitted from the fact that mummies were discovered in the two countries. They are exactly similar, and they are not Egyptian—for they lack the stone sarcophagi, the hieroglyphics, and the mummy-cloths. The mummies of Peru and Teneriffe are bound in skins of animals (a custom nowhere else found, although it is recorded of the Scythians)—those of the former in the skin of the lama, those of the latter in the skin of the goat, an animal in which the island abounded, and with the skins of which the original inhabitants clothed themselves. The mummies of both countries are also bound within the skins by leather thongs and straps, made from the hides of the respective animals. Such facts can not be accidental—they must be identical. The manner ascribed above may have been the custom in Mexican-America. That they are only discovered at Arica, in Peru, may arise from natural causes, viz., that at Arica the rain never falls (as in Egypt) and the soil is calcareous. The dryness of the atmosphere, with the saline qualities of the earth, produce natural embalming, thus preserving the bodies for ages from decomposition; while in other portions of the continent, from the moisture and the absence of preserving qualities, the bodies would gradually decay and return and mingle with the undistinguished dust of centuries.

There are points of similarity to the Tyrians observable in the details and decorations of the Peruvian mummies, both of the rich and the poor. Those of the poor are invariably found resting upon beds of broken fish-shells; those beds are supposed to have been placed there from religious motives. May not the purple murex (*i. e.*, dye-shellfish) of Tyrus (as on the altar of Copan) be here alluded to? In the same mummy pits (and they extend over a mile) are found models of boats, lines, and fish-hooks. These are buried with the mummies, and evidently are witnesses of the occupation or the religious motives of the departed! Is not Tyrus here, also? Her fisheries were her national emblems. And that this custom (whereby the means of sustenance were obtained) was practised in South America by the aborigines is distinctly stated by Dr. Robertson upon the authority of Berrere. The statement also shows that the distinction between the aborigines of the north and south, or Mexican America, is apparent; those of the former depended upon hunting for their sustenance, those of the latter, or the Tyrian descendants, as did their ancestors, upon their fisheries. Robertson says: "In this part of the globe (*i. e.*, South America) hunting seems not to have been the first employment of men, nor the first effort of their invention and labor to obtain food. They were fishers before they became hunters."—Vol. V., Book IV., p. 318.

The boat model is directly emblematical of a religious custom of Tyrus—copied from the Egyptian—viz., the belief that the soul has to pass through various stages and transitions before it reaches its final destination or happiness. To accomplish this, the body must pass over a river in a sacred barge or boat; the helmsman was called by the Egyptians, in their own language, Charon. The classic reader will instantly trace the mythological fable of Greece concerning the ferryman of the River Styx—probably introduced into Grecian Thebes by the Tyrian Cadmus.

The mummies of the rich discovered in Peru are invariably wrapped in cloth, crimson (purple) colored. Here, then, is the national color of Tyrus (derived from the shell-fish) and which made that country so renowned. This color is found enveloping the bodies of the rich, while the useless and "broken shells" of the fish are found beneath those of the poor—*the same national tribute to both* (though in degree according to the wealth of the deceased), for the Tyrians, like the Egyptians, admitted no distinction in the grave based upon rank or title—but held that good deeds alone constituted the true claim to distinction.

In a notice of the ancient mummies of Teneriffe, Alexander von Humboldt states that they differ from the Egyptians in physiognomy, and that the ornaments resemble those used in Mexican America. When the illustrious traveler wrote those facts (as shown in the following quotation) there was no theory in his mind in reference to the Tyrians—yet his remarks will support this present history, and they are too important, as to undeniable authority, to be passed by indifferently by the reader. Humboldt says: "On examining carefully the physiognomy of the ancient Canarians, able anatomists have recognized in the cheek-bones and the lower jaw a perceptible difference from the Egyptian mummies. The corpses are often decorated with small laces (necklaces) to which are hung little disks of baked earth (clay) that seemed to have served as numerical (religious?) signs; and resemble the quippoes of the *Peruvians and Mexicans.*"

Here, then, upon the high authority of Humboldt, is an analogy traced both by the ornaments of the mummies of the Guanches (Tyrians) and the ancient inhabitants of Mexican America. Upon every consideration of the subject, the mummies discovered at Teneriffe and in Peru are identical, the same kind are not found in any other parts of the world, and Teneriffe (as chief of the Fortunate Isles) was known, visited, and inhabited by the Tyrians.

After this long extract from Mr. Jones' history of ancient America, we will in the following lines consider the state of culture in ancient America as a relic of the ancient culture of mankind, which was preserved by its withdrawal from the development of the rest of the world to the fifteenth century.

When the Spaniards discovered America, they found people there, especially in three States, who were in some respects more cultivated than themselves, *i. e.*, the Aztecs, in Mexico or Anahuak; the Muyscas, on the high table-lands of Bogota, and the Peruvians in Peru. The latter state, and also the Mexican, had suffered many revolutions; that of the Muyscas, on the contrary, was of great antiquity in its existent condition. There immigrated into Mexico from the north, according to tradition, about the year 648, A.D., the nation of Toltec, who subjugated the former cultivated inhabitants and adopted their civilization, but finally was almost destroyed by internal dissension, pestilence, and other disasters. Afterwards there invaded Anahuak, about 1170, from the same region, the hunting nation of the Chichimecs, who had affinity with the Toltecs in language, and drove the remainder of their predecessors in government toward the south. These were followed by the Nahuatlacs, a family of Aztecs, established in 1325, on an island in the Lake Tezcuco the city of Tenochtitlan or Mexico. (The name Mexico denotes the residence of Mexitli or Huitzilopochtli, the mighty god of war of the Aztecs.) It was surrounded by five lakes and volcanoes. The Aztecs, gaining immense strengh, conquered all the southern countries as far as Guatemala, and the northern as far as Sonora. The last empire of the Peruvians is said to have arisen only in the twelfth century. All nations and empires mentioned here left behind them remarkable monuments of architecture and other arts. But all the rest are not to be compared to those of the most ancient and the most cultivated nation, the Maja people, who, long before the invasion of the Toltecs, were diffused over the continent and the islands. Their cities, whose prodigious ruins we find in Yucatan, Chiapa, Guatemala, and other countries, existed partially at the time of the Spanish dominion. The Teocallis (houses of God) and arched constructions near Kabah, the ruins of Labnah, with double columns, those of Zayi, with columns of almost Doric order, and those of Chiche, with large ornamental pilasters, were a certain proof of a high culture. It was owing to that circumstance that they were preserved from total destruction, because they differed especially in the fine arts, architecture and sculpture, from the Aztec cities. In regard to the similarity of these artificial works with those of the ancient Oriental, we will cite several observations of a decided opponent of a foreign origin of ancient American culture mentioned by Professor Müller. He says: "It is astonishing to every one to contemplate in the images the similarity in regard to decoration with the Egyptian, Etruscan, and Pelasgian ones."

Tiedeman classes these monuments of architecture with the Egyptian, Syrian, Persian, and Indian. Stephens found near Palenque a statue eleven and a half feet high, which in appearance was completely Egyptian. This latter is certainly a remarkable witness to the assumed fact that America was very early settled by a strange nation.

In Peru, especially on the banks of the large lake of Titicaca, which has an extent of over two hundred and forty square miles, existed a very ancient culture, whose monuments were lately examined by D'Orbigny. Among them were great statues of basalt, with heads like those of the Egyptians. In fact, one has only to look at the different American sculptures, as represented in the works of Squier, to be instantly struck with the similarity to the Egyptian statues, as well in the form of the pedestals as in the posture of the figures and the whole manner of representation. Especially prominent in this respect are the Teocallis (the houses of gods), or ancient Mexican pyramids, which were at once temples and monuments. They differ very much in magnitude and style, but resemble in their general features the pyramids of the Babylonians and Etruscans. In almost every age, until the Mexican race was conquered, such Teocallis existed. Some of them, and indeed precisely the most magnificent ones, are of the earliest age; for example, the pyramid of Cholula, which, according to tradition, was reared by the aborigines of Otomies.

Of this Alexander von Humboldt says: "It is impossible to read the descriptions which Herodotus and Diodorus Siculus have left us of the Temple of Belus, without being surprised at the similarity between it, as there described, and the Teocallis of Anahuak."

On the Mexican pyramids, as well as on the Bel temple, the workmanship of the interior—Naos—can be distinguished from that on the platform of the pyramid. This is plainly stated in the letters of Cortez.

Diodorus relates: "The Babylonian temple was used by the Chaldeans as an observatory." The Mexican priests likewise observed the position of the heavenly bodies from the turrets of the Teocallis, and proclaimed with hoarse cries through their trumpets the watches of the night.

Humboldt writes: "It does not appear from the ancient authors whether the sides of the temple of Bel, like the pyramids of the Egyptians and Americans, faced the four quarters of heaven." This matter is now, however, through the late investigation of Fresnels in Babylonia, reduced to a certainty.

The temple of Bel is by Diodorus called "the monument of Bel." By the Mexicans as by the Egyptians the pyramids were used as monuments.

In regard to magnitude, the pyramid of Cholula was very similar to that of the Egyptians. It was higher than the pyramid of Myserinos—twice as high as the one of Cheops.

It may be interesting to introduce a description of these monuments of architecture from Mr. Jones' "History of Ancient America."—Vol. I., pp. 51–54.

"The several discoveries of the ruined cities will now be reviewed and established. In the ancient capital of the Mexican Empire it has been stated that the Spaniards acted the character of incendiaries. In 1520, every available specimen of Mexican art was consumed by Cortez and the priests. Paintings, the only manuscripts of the Mexican nation, were destroyed and became a bonfire for the soldiery—every palace and temple of the capital was leveled to the earth, and the foundation of the first cathedral of the invaders was laid with thousands of statues—the idols of the aborigines. Every vestige of the Mexican records was supposed to have been consumed, broken, or burned. After a lapse of two hundred and seventy years, two statues were dug up in the grand plaza of the modern city of Mexico ; but from the interest felt for those religious relics by the poor descendants of the aborigines, the Spaniards secretly buried them, it was said, in the garden-court of a convent. At the same time (1790) was exhumed a circular piece of sculpture, having reference to the astronomical calendar of the ancient inhabitants, which is still preserved in Mexico."

A brief review of the discovery of the ruins and their locality will now be required. From a record by Huarros of Guatemala, and that on the authority of Fuentes, the ruins of Copan were known in 1700. Palenque was visited by Del Rio and by Dupaix about

1805. In the beginning of the nineteeth century the scientific Humboldt visited Mexico; he obtained drawings of the ruins of Mitla, in the province of Oaxaca, and others of a similar character, but especially of the terraced pyramid of Cholula, which he visited. The investigations were published by the same scholastic traveler. At a later period Uxmal (Yucatan) was explored under commission of the Spanish government, by Waldeck; his work (folio) is most beautifully illustrated. In compliment to the nobleman who published the great work of ancient Mexican paintings, he called one of the ruins "The Pyramid of Kingsborough"—an anachronism, perhaps allowable, when the motive is considered. Copan was visited by Galindo in 1836; but he lacked the perseverance necessary for a perfect exploration. This latter desideratum was fully evinced by Stephens and Catherwood, who, in 1839–40, visited and explored all of the above (excepting those seen by Baron Humboldt), and several cities before unknown in general history. As a geograpical position the localities of these dead cities are between the capital of Mexico and the Isthmus of Darien, but chiefly in Guatemala, on the borders of Yucatan and on that peninsula; they therefore occupy the narrow part of the continent between the two great oceans. A reference to the map of Central America will aid the following remarks:

The River Montagua empties itself into the Bay of Honduras, at or near Omoa; approaching the source of this river, it branches off to the south, which branch is called Copan River; above the rapids of this branch river is situated, on the banks, the now celebrated ruined city of Copan, over two miles in extent, parallel with the stream. Palenque is nearer Mexico. The ruins of Uxmal are in Yucatan. From the architectural characteristics of the edifices, we find no difficulty in arranging the order of their being built; which, with all due respect for the opinion of others, we submit to be as follows, viz.: first, the city of Copan, then Cholula, followed by Quirigua, Tezpan, Guatemala, Quiché, Gueguetinanga, Ocosingo, Mitla, Palenque, and lastly Uxmal; and about the same period of building, the cities of Chi-Chen, Zayi, Kabah, Espita and Ticol—these being in the peninsula of Yucatan.

The ruins necessary to be described for the illustration of our present subject, will be those of Copan, Palenque, and Uxmal, and for this purpose extracts will be quoted from the lately-published work on Central America by Mr. Stephens. These extracts will be given as unquestionable authority, and the engravings in the work will be received as accurate representations of the ruins, and upon which many of our results have been founded. On the subject of their accuracy, the fascinating traveler writes as follows:

"I will only remark, that from the beginning our great object and effort was to procure true copies of the originals, adding nothing for effect as pictures. Mr. Catherwood made the outline of all the drawings with the camera-lucida, and divided his paper into sections, so as to preserve the utmost accuracy of proportion. The engravings were made with the same regard to truth, from drawings reproduced by Mr. C. himself, the originals being also in the hands of the engraver. Proofs of every plate were given to Mr. C., who made such corrections as were necessary: and in my opinion, they are as true copies as can be presented, and except the stones themselves the reader can not have better materials for speculation and study."

Not only the monuments in stone testify to great antiquity, but also the hieroglyphic book. Like those of the Egyptian, the letters of the Mexicans denoted either things or ideas. They had also phonetic signs. There is in Dresden a still entirely inexplicable hieroglyphic writing, which resembles only the lapidary inscription discovered in Palenque, which Prescott regards as a phonetic writing. This kind of writing had attained among the Mexicans such a degree of perfection that even the proceedings at law (as by the Egyptians) were recorded thereby, and under the Spanish government public papers in hieroglyphic writing long obtained a legal value.

We have before mentioned (page 64) the lately discovered hieroglyphics in Taragona. Alexander von Minutoli gives pictures of them. These have certainly a similarity to the Egyptian ones, and in form resemble so much the Mexican, that we are compelled to regard them as a medium between the two species of hieroglyphics. The hieroglyphics of the ancient Mexicans give us an explanation of their tolerably perfect chronology. They had a solar year more perfect than that of the modern Europeans before the calendar reform. Like the Egyptians, they completed the year by five complementary days, and besides this intercalated after each cycle of fifty-two years, twelve and a half, or after one hundred and four years, twenty-five days, which brought them almost to the exact length of the tropical year.

In the same manner the old Persians, as Alexander von Humboldt affirms, inserted after the expiration of one hundred and twenty years (each of 365 days) a month of thirty days. The Etruscans had corresponding cycles of one hundred and ten years. A remarkable conformity between the Egyptian and ancient American calendar, Iomard proved in his letters, to which Alexander von Humboldt refers in his "Vues de Cordillères."

Still more marked is the coincidence between the oldest forms of government on the old and new continents.

It is known that the foundation of both was a hierarchy or sacerdotal monarchy. In Peru as well as in Egypt the king was worshipped as the Sun-God. In Mexico the nobility possessed the greatest power after the king. On their vast estates they ruled over the peasantry, who belonged to them. Sentence was pronounced by regular judges, and wholly independent courts of justice held by them. The priests shared this power. Of these Prescott (Vol. I., p. 54) says:

"The sacerdotal order was very numerous, as may be inferred from the statement that five thousand priests were, in some way or other, attached to the principal temple in the capital. The various ranks and functions of this mnltitudinous body were discriminated with great exactness. Those best instructed in music took the management of their choirs. Others arranged the festivals conformably to the calendar. Others superintended the education of the youth, and others had charge of the hieroglyphical paintings and oral traditions, while the dismal rites of sacrifice were reserved for the chief dignitaries of the order. At the head of the whole establishment were two high-priests, elected from the order, as it would seem, by the king and principal nobles, without reference to birth, but solely for their qualifications as shown by their previous conduct in a subordinate station. They were equal in dignity and inferior only to the sovereign, who rarely acted without their advice in weighty matters of public concern.

"The priests were each devoted to the service of some particular deity, and had quarters provided within the spacious precincts of their temple, at least while engaged in immediate attendance there—for they were allowed to marry and have families of their own. In this monastic residence they lived in all the stern severity of conventual discipline. Thrice during the day and once at night they were called to prayers. They were frequent in their ablutions and vigils, and mortified the flesh by fasting and cruel penance—drawing blood from their bodies by flagellation and piercing them with the thorns of aloe; in short, by practising all those austerities to which fanaticism (to borrow the strong language of the poet) has resorted in every age of the world,

> "'In hopes to merit heaven by making earth a hell.'

The great cities were divided into districts, placed under the charge of a sort of parochial clergy, who regulated every act of religion within their precincts. It is remarkable that they administered the rites of confession and absolution. The secrets of the confessional were held inviolable, and penances were imposed of much the same kind as those enjoined in the Roman Catholic Church. There were two remarkable peculiarities in the Aztec ceremony. The first was, that as the repetition of an offense, once atoned for, was deemed inexpiable, confession was made but once in a man's life, and was usually deferred to a late period of it, when the penitent unburdened his conscience, and settled at once the long arrears of iniquity. Another peculiarity was, that priestly absolution was received in place of the legal punishment of offenses, and authorized an acquittal in case of arrest. Long after the conquest the simple natives, when they came under the arm of the law, sought to escape by producing the certificate of their confession.

"One of the most important duties of the priesthood was that of education, to which certain buildings were appropriated within the inclosure of the principal temple. Here the youth of both sexes of the higher and middling orders were placed at a very tender age. The girls were intrusted to the care of priestesses, for women were allowed to exercise sacerdotal functions except those of sacrifice. In these institutions the boys were drilled in the routine of monastic discipline; they decorated the shrines of the gods with flowers, fed the sacred fires, and took part in the religious chants and festivals. Those in the higher school—the Calmecan, as it was called—were initiated in their traditionary lore, the mysteries of hieroglyphics, the principles of government, and such branches of astronomical and natural science as were within the compass of priesthood. The girls learned various feminine employments, especially to weave and embroider rich coverings for the altars of the gods. Great attention was paid to the moral discipline of both sexes. The most perfect decorum prevailed, and offenses were punished with extreme rigor, in some instances with death itself. Terror, not love, was the spring of education with the Aztecs. At a suitable age for marrying, or for entering into the world, the pupils were dismissed with much ceremony from the convent, and the recommendation of the principal often introduced those most competent to responsible situations in public life. Such was the crafty policy of the Mexican priests, who, by reserving to themselves the business of instruction, were enabled to mould the young and plastic mind according to their own wills, and to train it early to implicit reverence for religion and its ministers; a reverence which still maintained its hold on the iron nature of the warrior, long after every other vestige of education had been effaced by the rough trade to which he was devoted.

"To each of the principal temples lands were annexed for the maintenance of the priests. These estates were augmented by the policy or devotion of successive princes, until under the last Montezuma, they had swollen to an enormous extent, and covered every district of the empire. The priests took the management of their property into their own hands, and they seem to have treated their tenants with the liberality and indulgence characteristic of monastic corporations. Besides the large supplies drawn from this source, the religious order was enriched with the first-fruits, and such other offerings as piety or superstition dictated. The surplus beyond what was required for the support of the national worship was distributed in alms among the poor; a duty strenuously prescribed by their moral code. Thus we find the same religion inculcating lessons of pure philanthropy, on the one hand, and of merciless extermination on the other. The inconsistency will not appear incredible to those who are familiar with the history of the Roman Catholic Church in the early ages of the Inquisition."

All this agrees substantially with what Diodorus, Herodotus, and others, relate of the authority, the duties, manners of living *of the Egyptian priests.* There is one difference, *i. e.*, the Mexican priests formed no caste. Therein, as in almost all things, they agreed with the Phœnicians and Carthaginians, who were likewise without any hereditary caste except that of the nobility.

No greater difference exists in the mythology. Stress has been laid upon the idea that the names of the ancient American gods are entirely different from those of the deities of Oriental antiquity. It may be proved that this is not exactly so, and even if the conformity had been brought about by accident, we can demonstrate that the counterproof resting upon the pretended variety is not a valid one.

The word for God—"teo"—teot—teotl—belongs to the primitive Indo-Germanic tongue, and with other Aric constituent parts of the ancient American languages, can be traced also in the above-mentioned Iranic colonies in North Africa and Spain. With the word "teo" many words are compounded—for instance, their holy book, "teoamoxtli"—the temple, "teocalli," etc. Their religion was founded, as among all nations of hierarchical proclivities, on the adoration of "Nature." They believed in an invisible and infinite Spirit, who was worshiped since the oldest times, though not by the mass of the people. The name of this highest god was, in the Mexican language, "Teotl;" in the Nicaraguic, "Teot," almost the same with the Phœnician "Taaut," and the Egyptian "Toit," "Teit," or "Tot." The author Philo Judæus regards the

"Taaut" as heaven or world, and the author Varro calls him "the highest god." The next deity among the Aztecs and Maja people was the goddess "Centeotl." Mr. Müller describes her (p. 491) in the following manner: "The Centeotl, an old oracle deity —she is the Ceres of the people, the goddess of maize at first, then, on account of the high appreciation of this cereal in America, the goddess of agriculture generally"—therefore the deity of culture of the aborigines. It is not to be wondered at, that this goddess of culture obtained a great cosmological estimation. She was called plainly "Toncajohua"—the nourisher of mankind. This cosmological appreciation led necessarily to a cosmogonic origin. So, also, "Centeotl" —the great progenitor—was not only the goddess of humanity, but she was "great, or primitive goddess." Therefore Clavigero considers her, without reason, identical with the goddess "Tonautzin." The best Spanish authors consider her identical with "Teteionan"—the mother of gods. Who would not be reminded hereby of the mother of all the gods, "Cybele." With this goddess and "Teteionan," the goddess "Taauthe" (likewise called mother of gods), was identical among nations cognate to the Phœnicians, *i. e.*, the Babylonians. She was represented standing upon a lion. In Carthage, "the heavenly origin," "the mother of gods," was a goddess of Nature, and especially of rain and procreation. Like the Centeotl in America she gave oracles, which were highly honored till the victory of Christianity. Centeotl is identical with "Astaroth" of the Phœnicians, whom Varro calls "the goddess of earth," and joins to the heavenly god "Taautes." The sacrifices offered to her were ears of corn and human beings. Human sacrifices were common through the whole of America, especially among the Aztecs.

As among the ancient Asatics, so also in ancient America were the moon (Tona or

Meztli), and the Sun (Tonatiuh) the chief gods. Corresponding to them are the Phœnician deities "Baalmoloch," and Tanais or Tanat. The worship of the former god is notorious on account of its abominable character. In Carthage and Phœnicia were statues of the god "Moloch," of ore, having in their interior a large excavation. Upon the extended red-hot hand of the idol, children were laid to roll down into the burning mouth. In 1518 the Spaniards, under Juan de Grijalva, found in Central America quite similar statues, erected for the purpose of human sacrifices. Humboldt says: "The god Tonatluh is represented with an opened mouth with armed teeth. This open mouth, widely extended tongue, remind us of Kala-Chronos, who swallowed his children, and whom we recognize among the Phœnicians under the name of *Moloch.*" Tonatiuh, placed in the midst of the signs of the day, when the year was measured by the motions of the solstices and equinox, is *the genuine symbol of time.* That Tonatiuh is identical with the Phœnician "Moloch" appears also from the fact that to the one as well as the other were stone columns erected (as symbols of the ascending flames) in order to indicate the position of the "Sun." Next to the Sun-god appears the "Moon," among the Phœnicians and Carthaginians as well as on the Antilles. Among the former nations it was worshiped by the name of Tanat or Tanit, in America by the name of Tona. This close verbal resemblance between the names is the more important, as Mr. Müller places the "Tona" by herself as a primitive goddess of the Maja people.

The Caribbeans, who represented the Phœnicians in America, were a widely diffused race, a vigorous although rude nation. They frequented all the coasts of Central America in large vessels, and even carried on some commerce. They possessed a whiter skin and nobler features than most of the other aborigines. This was, perhaps, in consequence of a mingling of Semites with the aborigines of the Guarani race (an afterward degenerated nation). This race believed in a supreme god, "Chemun" or "Chemeen," of whom it is related that he destroyed his worshipers by a deluge because they offered him only meagre sacrifices. This fact likens him to the Phœnician Baal-Chamman, whom Philo calls "Pontus," or god of the ocean.

By no other nation, not even by the ancient Egyptians, were the dreams of the astrologer so blindly relied upon. He was immediately called in at the birth of a child. The time of the event was accurately ascertained, and the family was waiting with trembling attention, while the servant of heaven unfolded the destiny of the infant from the dark book of fate. Who does not call to mind here the astrology of the Chaldeans and the later Asiatics?

As with us the signs of the zodiac bear the names of animals, so also in ancient America.

The Great Bear was known among the Indians by the very same name.

The worship of animals has always been combined with the worship of the stars. Ever since the names of animals were given to the stars, the veneration of these has been transferred to the animals diffused over all parts of ancient America.

Very remarkable it is, that on both continents almost the same animals were considered sacred. In America the Ape was venerated, as it was among the Carthaginians. The Scorpion, the Eagle, the Lion, the Bear, as in nearly all ancient Asia. On both continents the gods were represented with heads of animals. In Egypt "Toit," with that of a sparrowhawk. The Phœnician "Moloch" with that of an ox; and among the Mexicans the god of war, "Huitzilipochtli," bore the head of a sparrow. The Serpent was especially venerated. The mythologies of both continents embrace a multitude of serpentine gods. Among the Egyptians the "Kneph;"

among the Aztecs the "Coatlicon;" among the Olemians "Mixcoatl," their principal god. "Wotan," of whom we shall speak hereafter, had a serpentine body and hawk's head, like "Kneph" and "Agathodemon."

There are numerous monuments of a primitive civilization, which perished long ago, scattered over America in the form of animals. One of the most remarkable of these is a mound in the State of Ohio, which Andree describes in the following manner:

"In Adams county, Ohio, stands, near the Brush Creek, on a hill one hundred and fifty feet above the level of the sea, a large mound of a snake-like appearance, the head on one end of the elevation, the body wound in a pleasing manner, having a length of seven hundred feet, the end of the tail in a threefold curl. The mouth is wide open, before and partially in it lies an oblong figure resembling an egg." This mysterious monument can only be explained and accounted for in the light of Oriental antiquity. The

Egyptians and Phœnicians believed that the world proceeded out of the mouth of the creator, and was symbolized by them as an egg. The American hill represents, therefore, nothing else than the *creation of the world.* The world-snake was called among the Egyptians "Kneph," by which they also meant the galaxy, which, like a boa-constrictor, embraces the celestial globe. Beside the galaxy appears also the constellation of the dragon, clasping the heavens as a sign of the serpentine worship. The snake signified, symbolically, Time. Among the Egyptians Sevac, or Chronos, was represented as a snake, and was sometimes called "Dahaka," which means a serpent. It is remarkable that with the Mexicans, also, the hieroglyphic sign for the idea of Time was a snake.

The American aborigines, like the nations of the old world, held the doctrine of the immortality of the soul. They believed in a future condition of joy, and also in an inferior state, where souls wandered through strange constellations or lived in bodies either of noble or common animals, ruled by governors both male and female.

Our frequent references have already shown that the similarity of the American and Oriental antiquities has not remained unperceived. It strikes even those who agree with those scholars, Müller and Andree, whom we have often quoted, who pertinaciously maintain the dogma of the indigenous origin of the American culture. They, however, find the cause of that conformity in the unity of the human race and the common nature of the human spirit. This theory we believe to have been refuted.

One can readily conceive that the veneration of the sun, moon, and the whole order of nature, might have originated and existed with nations having no connection with each other; that these nations might independently have given names of animals to constellations, and have had hieroglyphic and phonetic writings—but we can not understand why, by reason of mere unity of the race and the common origin of human spirit, the gods in America and Asia should bear the very same names, the constellations be represented by the very same animals, and the serpent be the symbol of Time on both sides of the Atlantic Ocean.

Mr. Müller repeats an account, according to which the companions of Juan de Grijalva, in 1518, found a marble lion on an island, to which were offered fumigations and human sacrifices; he forgets, however, that in Central America there are no lions, and that in South America there exists only a single species of lions, *i. e.*, the Pumas, which still more resemble cats than the lions of the old continent. It is well known, however, that the lion among all people of the hierarchical period, especially among the Phœnicians and Carthaginians, was very highly honored. These legends belong partly to the oldest period of the ancient traditions of mankind, and became, as it frequently is with traditions, connected with their local legends; partly they are certain reports of ancient immigrations from a far country beyond the Atlantic Ocean.

The well-known Greek myth of the Son of Apollo setting the globe on fire by misdriving his father's chariot, symbolizes a disturbance of the constellations, which, according to their idea, revolved around the earth, and a consequent destruction of the world by fire. The Greeks had also a tradition of the ocean deities sweeping it with a deluge. Among all the nations of the old world we find like beliefs, and also the one concerning the four periods of the world. In America we meet with them likewise. The Etruscans, Persians, and East Indians considered these periods to be of three thousand years' duration.

Humboldt gives, in his "Vues des Cordillères et Monumens des peuples indigènes de l'Amérique" (Paris, 1810), the duration of the world as 18,028 years, divided into four cycles. The first cycle, or the age of giants, of 5,206 years; the second cycle, or the age of fire, of 4,804; the third cycle, or the age of winds, of 4,010; the fourth cycle, or the age of water, of 4,008.

The Mexican tradition of the deluge says: "The grandfather of Wotan saved himself and his family in a boat, and afterward his grandson, Wotan, assisted in the erection of a huge building by which it was proposed to reach heaven. This scheme was interrupted. Each family took a different language, and the Great Spirit commanded Wotan to go to Anahuak (Mexico) and people it." Here we have the exact Biblical account.

Humboldt calls attention to the fact, that Buddha in the Indian—Wodansday in Germany—both denote the first day of a small period, (week), and among the inhabitants of Chiapa the Wednesday (after Wotan) was the first day of a cycle of five days.

The Indian Buddha and the German Wodan

bear a similar relation to the deluge with that of the Mexican Wotan. The German Wodan himself caused the deluge by slaying a giant whose blood overflowed the world. The Indian Buddha is the son of Manu, who, with the seven Rishis, escaped in a vessel. This legend resembles the American one mentioned by Humboldt. He tells us: "The people were metamorphosed into fish, except seven who fled into caverns. When the waters disappeared one of these giants, named Xelhua—the architect—went to Cholula, where he erected for a memorial on the mountain Tlaloc, that had served him and his companions as a refuge, an artificial hill of pyramidal form. He caused bricks to be made in the province of Tlamanalca, and in order to transport them to Cholula placed a row of men between these places, who passed them from hand to hand. The gods saw with anger this building, which was intended to reach to heaven, and threw fire upon it. Many laborers perished, and for the future it was consecrated to the god of air, Quetzalcoatl." According to the tradition of Edda (a collection of poems exhibiting the Runic or Scandinavian mythology, philosophy, etc.), all the giants of primitive times were drowned in the blood of the Ymir, except Bergelmir, who was saved in a chest. We have here as well as in Mexico giants flourishing at the time of the deluge. The giants who escaped, Bergelmir and Xelhua, show even similarity of name, as "gelmir" is a word by itself, signifying "ancient." In the tradition of Cholula, Xelhua rears the gigantic building with Wotan for his assistant. In like manner, the Germanic Wodan builds after the deluge the god's castle "Asgard" from the eyebrows of the slain giant. The coincidence of the number seven of the persons saved with the seven "Rishis" of the Indian legend, is also very striking. Such manifold analogies certainly can not arise from mere accident. In fine, without distorting the most simple and undeniable facts we can not deny the identity of the American Wotan with the German Wodan and the Indian Buddha. They agree,

1. In name.
2. In giving a name to a day of the week.
3. In their connection with the great deluge.
4. In assisting in the the erection of magnificent buildings after its subsidence.

Lastly—Being genealogic chiefs.

It is known that from the Indian Buddha the whole, so named, moon sect was derived. In Germany princes and nobles boasted of their descent from Wodan; and in America there existed, even in the sixteenth century, professed descendants of Wotan. In the discussion of the Indian word "Teo" for God, we called attention to a possible origin of various Aric elements in the language and culture of ancient America from Aric colonies of Northern Africa, mentioned by Sallust and others. The religious myths indicate, also, a Phœnician origin.

Traditions of the deluge are common to both continents. The European discoverers of America met them everywhere. Even the wild hordes of the Iroquois and Ojibeways preserved a tradition of a great flood, in which the Great Spirit had destroyed all the human race except a single family. Among these legends is one especially remarkable, of which Mr. Müller gives the following abstract: "The ancient nation of Nahuatlacs, denominated as Tezpi (their Noah) him who escaped the deluge. According to them he filled his boat with various animals. As the waters decreased he sent out a vulture, which did not return, because it found nourishment in the corpses of the giants. Afterward he sent a humming-bird, who came back with a twig in his beak." The resemblance of this legend to the Asiatic ones appears clearly. Of those of the Phœnicians we know little but that they were analogous to those of the cognate Jews and Babylonians. As we have seen, legends of both continents assert the erection after the deluge of a great tower. The Babylonian one, Alexander Eratosthenes, the polyhistorian, relates in this way: "All the people assembled and built a great tower in order to ascend to heaven. The Almighty God however destroyed the tower by storms, and allotted to every man a different language, for which reason their city was called Babylon."

We have already narrated the Mexican legend, according to which the giant Xelhua having reared the great pyramid of Cholula in order to reach heaven, the gods became enraged at his audacity, threw fire upon his work, and gave to each human family a separate language. In connection with this must be remembered the similarity of the pyramidal temple, which we must believe to be the tower mentioned by the polyhistorian, and to which the Mexican pyramids, especially those of Cholula, had the greatest similarity.

The most important, however, of the American traditions are those which speak distinctly of an immigration from the East. Mr. Jones says: "The Spanish historian, Sahagan, who lived on friendly terms with the aborigines for sixty years, and wrote only fifteen years after the Cortezian conquest, relates, on the authority of Montezuma, who gave the tradition as from the remotest times —it was also proved by historical paintings —that their ancestors, as a colony, first touched at Florida, then crossed or coasted the Gulf of Mexico and Yucatan, and finally landed and settled somewhere on the shores of the Bay of Honduras." The same author, moreover, writes: "The wreck of an ancient galley has been found in Mexican America, deeply imbedded in the sands. Now, this must have been the remains of a Phœnician vessel, for the Greeks and Romans had no galleys on the Atlantic waters, or even the Indian Ocean, until the time of Alexander, but the Tyrians had, and nearly one thousand years before the Christian era." The ancient Americans were very modest in regard to their intellectual possessions, for they did not pretend to have acquired their culture by themselves, but on the contrary, positively affirmed that they owed it to foreigners of white complexion. Since the Indians, like the Moguls, are copper-colored, their obligation to immigrants of the Caucasian race is plainly expressed by this story. Mr. Müller gives the Peruvian tradition as follows:

"In the beginning men lived as barbarians, without law and social order, or desire for other nourishment than that which Nature offered. The Sun had pity on people in this miserable condition, and sent two of his children, Manco Capac (Capac signified great or powerful) and his sister Mamma Oello, to introduce civilization and the worship of the Sun among them. A golden perch was to go before Manco and his sister and enter into the ground at their proper place of residence. The perch pointed out the region of Cuzco, a place whose name signifies 'navel.' After this Manco Capac and Mamma Oello went out in all directions, ordered the worship of the Sun, abolished human sacrifices and cannibalism, and persuaded the wild hordes to accept civilization, to study the arts and sciences, to enter into matrimony, to establish laws, build cities and villages, make roads and aqueducts," etc. Montesinos, a distinguished antiquarian who lived fifteen years in Peru, puts Manco Capac in the most ancient times, while others fix upon the eleventh century as the period of his flourishing. The opinion of Montesinos, however, is confirmed by numerous monuments.

The legend of the Muyscas, on the tableland of Bogota, relating to this runs thus: "In the first times, when the moon did not yet exist, the people of Muyscas were barbarians, without agriculture, without religion, without manners, without government. Then appeared a bearded and very aged man from the East who had three names, 'Bochica,' 'Namquethala,' and 'Zuhe,' and three heads. He taught the barbarians how to wear clothes, how to cultivate the fields, how to worship gods, how to form states."

The belief in an immigration of foreigners from across the Atlantic Ocean as at the time of the Spanish conquest was so common among the Mexicans, that it even exerted a great influence on the destruction of their empire at that time, for they believed the Spaniards to be the descendants of the hero "Quetzalcoatl," come again to claim their own. He was a white and bearded man from the East, like the Bochica of the Muyscas, a lawgiver, and high-priest at Tula. After having governed for a long time in Tula, and then in Cholula, in such a way that the time of his rule was remembered by the people of Anahuak as the golden age, he embarked at the mouth of the Goazocoalcos River (which still forms the single safe harbor on the Mexican coast) and departed with the promise to return one day with his descendants.

Prescott says: "That day was looked forward to with hope or with apprehension, according to the interest of the believer, but with general confidence throughout the wide borders of Anahuak."

Just at the time of Montezuma this conviction was strengthened by preternatural signs —the appearance of comets, the conflagration of a temple, the overflow of the great lake of Tezcuco, etc. Fernando Cortez made use of this belief with great ingenuity. The white skin of his followers, their long beards, the thunder and lightning in their hands, and especially their arrival in wonderful vessels from countries beyond the ocean, so strengthened even Montezuma in the opinion of their descent from Quetzalcoatl, that he, thus far the sovereign master of the richest and most beautiful empire of the continent, yielded almost voluntarily to Cortez. During his interview with the Spaniard he himself said to him: "We know through our books that our ancestors were not aborigines, but were led here by a great Being who afterward withdrew to the regions of the sunrise. When he returned to seek those who had settled here, he found them married to the women of this country, having a numerous posterity and living in cities built by themselves. They did not wish longer to obey their former master, and he departed alone; but we have always trusted that his descendants would come to assume his empire. As you come from the Orient, I can not doubt that the king who has sent you is our natural lord."

These words one may compare with the passages of Plutarch, which we again quote (page 22).

§ 5. "On the continent Hellenians live around the bay which is not smaller than the Palus Mæotis (Sea of Azof.)

§ 6. "They believe that the attendants of Hercules had allied themselves with the people of Chronos, and had reinflamed, invigorated, and enlarged the Greek character, which had been almost extirpated by barbarian language, laws, and manner of living. Therefore Hercules has the greatest honors, but Chronos the next."

Here are two accounts of the same matter coming from two different nations separated by a space of more than fourteen hundred years. Both speak of America as before inhabited, and as having been taken possession of by a nation coming from the East. Both mention a great chieftain of the colonists, whom Plutarch calls "Hercules." Hercules left behind his companions on the western continent as the Mexican hero left the forefather of Montezuma. According to Plutarch, the companions of Hercules mingled with a so-called nation of Chronos, and revived a rapidly declining culture. According to the Mexicans, the chief of the emigrants on his return found his people married to the women of the country, with numerous descendants in cities built by themselves.

This perfect coincidence determines the truth of both traditions. Plutarch's gulf, not smaller than the Palus Mæotis, and surrounded by a continent tallies exactly with the Gulf of Mexico. We said already that those settlers called Greeks by Plutarch were undoubtedly another race.

It is especially remarkable that both traditions assert not only a discovery of America, but also a colozination, which agrees with the proved similarity of the systems of culture of the old and new continents, and with the typical affinity of many American nations with the Semitic race. The Phœnicians alone must not be considered in this connection, but also the remaining people on the shores of the Mediterranean; as, for instance, the Etruscans (who are mentioned by Strabo in relating the Great Atlantic discovery), and especially the Spaniards. Not to speak of the hieroglyphics discovered in Tarragona, already mentioned (page 64), we notice the similarity of the development of the Basque language to that of the American original languages, to which Vater refers in "Mithridates, oder allgemeine Sprachenkunde" (Berlin, 1812), and which is spoken in the Spanish Basque provinces Alàva, Guipuscoa, and Biscaya.

From the eleventh till near the seventh century B.C., the greater part of Spain was a province of Tyre, whose merchants ruled there as the English once did in India. To this, the most prosperous period of Phœnician power, is to be referred, according to the intimations of Diodorus, the ancient discovery of America. The Carthaginian discovery of which Aristotle speaks can consequently be understood as induced by the recollection of the first discovery. This is not to be dated later than the sixth century B.C. At that time the power of the Etruscans decreased very much, and the country now called Cisalpine Gaul, which had belonged entirely to them, was conquered by the Gauls. By the same nation, perhaps, their dominion in Spain was destroyed. Since the pouring of such a mass of Celts into Spain and Italy was doubtless followed by the flight of many of the former inhabitants, an immigration on their part to a far western country is rendered at least probable. Some such measure was almost a necessity after the over-populating of the countries near the Mediterranean Sea.

The statement of Diodorus is also worthy of note, that the Carthaginians had intended, in case of a great misfortune, to emigrate to that island. Perhaps the story of Plutarch concerning the American who visited the eastern continent and remained for a long time among the ruins of Carthage, so far as it deserves any consideration, may refer to a descendant of such an emigrant Carthaginian.

We now turn to examine briefly several arguments against an immigration to America.

The most prominent is the great variety of languages showing no similarity with the known elements of tongues, and having substantial differences among themselves. The Basque language forms only an isolated exception. There are eight hundred and sixty languages spoken on the globe, enumerated by a philologist, and four hundred and twenty-three of them were counted in America. The American languages are, however, far from having been completely investigated, and the investigation loses much of its importance in consequence of the tradition that at the time of the Phœnician settlement in America there were already inhabitants there. That the language of these primitive people would gain the superiority in the amalgamation is the easier to believe as, according to Plutarch and Montezuma, the immigrants having no women married the aboriginal women. The children of these marriages would incline to the language of their mothers rather than to that of their fathers, as may be observed in our day. At the present time in America, the European languages are frequently subdued by the Indian —the Spanish in Bolivia and Peru, the Portuguese in San Paolo by the indigenous Guarani. Besides, even Plutarch says (page 22, par. 6), that the attendants of Hercules mingled themselves with the people of Chronós, and being left behind, inflamed, invigorated, and enlarged again the Greek character, which had been almost extinguished by barbarian language, laws, and manners of living. Other arguments are drawn from the Indian ignorance of iron and draught animals. But throughout the ancient world iron was little used, and in its place were employed copper and the more precious metals. Domestic animals were not easily to be conveyed in the vessels of the ancients across the ocean. America possesses only two original kinds of cattle, the "bison" and the "musk ox," which are brought under the yoke with great difficulty, and in spite of the luxuriance of pasture yield but little milk. Finally, it is urged that when a savage and a civilized race are brought face to face in a country, the former may be crushed or melt away before the latter, but never becomes civilized. But we must remember the great distinction between the Europeans of our day, who, by reason of their too high culture, have lost the ability to treat barbarians in the proper way, and these hierarchical nations of antiquity.

According to the Indian traditions, it was priests who brought them their culture, and the example of the Jesuitical state, "Paraguay," furnishes us proof from modern history that through the influence of priests barbarians have been known to acquire civilization. Besides, it is by no means necessary to adopt the opinion that at the time of the arrival of the Phœnicians only savages existed in America. There are no objections to the theory of a prior immigration of the semi-cultivated Eastern Asiatics of the Mongolian race.

The people of ancient America and their culture offer among themselves such varieties, that the adoption of a theory of several immigrations from various regions of the world does not so much create as solve difficulties. Gützlaff, in his "History of the Chinese Empire," says, that just as a few years ago some miserable Japanese dshunkens, without oars or masts, were thrown by a storm upon the coast of California, so it could also have happened thousands of years ago. Chinese annals, at the time of the Emperor "Shihoangti" (the builder of the great wall, 246–210 B.C.), tell of islands far away in the ocean, on which grows the herb of immortality; and a few years ago the Chinese interpreter in San Francisco, a Mr. James Hanley, published in the journal "The True Union," extracts translated from Chinese histories, concerning a vast country by the name of "Fusang," lying twenty thousand leagues east of Japan, beyond the great ocean, and of which accounts were brought in 459 by five mendicant friars, who had visited it and distributed Buddhistic tracts and pictures among the inhabitants. The descriptions of the Chinese historians agree remarkably with those of the Spanish conquerors, both in regard to the state of the country and of the culture. Mr. Hanley directs attention to the similarity of many Chinese words to Indian ones—as Nang-hand, in Indian Nanga; Keok-foot, in Indian Keoka; Yuet-moon, in Indian Yueta; Yat, sun, in Indian Yeeta; Azpa, father—Ama, mother—in Indian also Azpa and Ama. Prescott maintains for the Mexican people called Othomies or Othomi (from "otho," stationary, and "mi," nothing), a similarity of language with the Chinese.

The most prominent proofs, however, Alexander von Humboldt draws from the mode of culture of ancient America. The Aztecs called, for instance, days and years after the same animals whose names are applied to the zodiac. This use of the names of animals was current in Eastern Asia.

Prescott says here: "A correspondence quite as extraordinary is found between the hieroglyphics used by the Aztecs as signs of the days, and those zodiacal signs which the Eastern Asiatics employed." We call the attention of the reader to an extract of Jones' "History of Ancient America," proving that the Mexican aborigines were originally from the Tyrians. He says, in Vol. I., pages 200–203:

"The following powerful analogies prove that the Mexican aborigines were originally from the Tyrians. The summary is as follows, viz.: Religious idolatry; the worship of, and sacrifice of human lives to the god of war; the worship of Saturn, and consequent infanticide to propitiate the remorseless deity; the long cross (and others) of the goddess Astarte; in the sculpture; the sacrifice to Hygeia by optional circumcision; the chief worship of Apollo or the sun; the gorgeous temples erected to his glory; human sacrifices upon the dedication of the temples, and the sacred fire guarded by the virgins of the sun; the comparative mummies of the Tyrian Isles and Peru; the traditional story concerning swans; the tortoise and serpent in sculpture; the dye-shell or purple murex; navigation, with its attendant maps and charts; the aborigines coming from the East and by navigation; their landing or touching at Florida and before the Christian era; then the discovery of a wreck of a Tyrian galley; the knowledge of painting and the general application of colors and gem engraving; (as the sculpture contains only hieroglyphics and not one cypher or letter, consequently the spoken language of Phœnicia is not found, nor is there any other language discovered, and for a proof of its antiquity the Tyrian temple-sculpture should be only hieroglyphical;) the political character in the formation of monarchies and republics, as shown at Tyrus and Carthage, Mexico and

Toltecas; military character and knowledge of defensive locality, with analogous architecture in the sea and river walls of Tyrus and Copan; the last event in the history of Tyrus sculptured upon the chief altar of the most ancient ruin (Copan), and from the character of that event it would naturally become the first subject of record in the country to which they had emigrated—every detail of that altar is essentially Tyrian; painted sculpture and the stuccoing of the walls of Tyrus and Palenque; the architecture, as to its square-columned style, identified as Tyrian, and proved to be analogous from the temples of Jerusalem and Palenque and from the square pillars of Copan; while the pyramidal base produced the compound term, Egypto-Tyrian.

"These absolute analogies have been traced from Holy Writ (and from that source others are to follow), histories and traditions; from sculpture, coins, and architecture, and the entire range of the arts;

earth and ocean have rendered their records to establish that the same knowledge and customs were possessed by both nations; nor will the proof of identity stop there; their mutual knowledge was also found in that science where heaven itself was and is the illuminated map of study; where the stars are as letters of fire from the language of the skies—God himself being the Alpha and the Omega!

"The sublime science of astronomy claims both Tyrus and Tyrian-America for her children and pupils. The latter viewed and solved the problem of the annual course of the glorious sun (the chief worship) with as much accuracy (save a diurnal fraction) as the later and more accomplished scholars and disciples—Italy, Germany, and England.

"We submit to the opinion even of a sceptical reader, whether he does not, with the foregoing proofs, believe our historical proposition, viz.: That Tyrians were the first inhabitants of ancient America, and the original builders of the now ruined cities and temples?"

It would be the greatest discovery in the history of mankind to find idioms which, with certain modifications, are used both in America and in the interior of Asia, or in which at least an old affinity could be perceived. Indeed, such a discovery would be received with the greatest enthusiasm. Analogies of languages deserve only to be relied upon when they consist not in similarities of sound of the radical words, but show themselves in the organic formation, in the etymological richness, and especially in that which is the production of the intellectual power of the human spirit, *i. e.*, the philosophy of the language. Let us confidently hope and trust that this philological discovery will ere long be made. For although sceptres break, weapons rust, the arms of heroes moulder, and even whole nations disappear from the theatre of life, that intellectual power with which our great Lord and Maker has gifted the human soul is forever new, forever progressing and creating.

THE END.

www.ingramcontent.com/pod-product-compliance
Lightning Source LLC
LaVergne TN
LVHW021416110826
845150LV00007B/1949

* 9 7 8 1 4 2 5 5 0 9 8 4 2 *